NATIONAL GEOGRAPHIC

CIVILIZATIONS PAST TO PRESENT

PERU

HELEN BYERS

PICTURE CREDITS
Cover Jeremy Horner/CORBIS; page 3 (top) William Allard/National Geographic Society Image Collection; page 3 (bottom) Index/Bridgeman Art Library; pages 4–5 Brian A. Vikander/CORBIS; pages 7 (top), 24 South American Pictures/Tony Morrison; page 7 (bottom) British Library, London, UK/Bridgeman Art Library; page 8 Phil Schermeister/CORBIS; pages 9, 21 Angelo Cavalli/The Image Bank/Getty Images; page 10 Craig Duncan/DDB Stock Photo; page 11 Craig Lovell/CORBIS; page 12 Michele Burgess/Index Stock Imagery/PictureQuest; page 13 The Image Bank/Getty Images; page 14 Courtesy of the Time Museum, Rockford, Illinois; page 15 H.R. Dorig/Hutchison Picture Library; page 16 Werner Forman/Art Resource, NY; page 17 (bottom) Danny Lehman/CORBIS; page 17 (top) American Museum of Natural History, New York/Bridgeman Art Library; page 18 Wolfgang Kaehler/CORBIS; page 19 Jorge Provenza/Art Resource, NY; page 20 South American Pictures/Bill Leimbach; page 22 (top) Dave G. Houser/CORBIS; page 22 (bottom) Don Mason/CORBIS.

Produced through the worldwide resources of the National Geographic Society, John M. Fahey, Jr., President and Chief Executive Officer; Gilbert M. Grosvenor, Chairman of the Board; Nina D. Hoffman, Executive Vice President and President, Books and Education Publishing Group.

PREPARED BY NATIONAL GEOGRAPHIC SCHOOL PUBLISHING
Ericka Markman, Senior Vice President and President, Children's Books and Education Publishing Group; Steve Mico, Vice President, Editorial Director; Marianne Hiland, Executive Editor; Anita Schwartz, Project Editor; Jim Hiscott, Design Manager; Kristin Hanneman, Illustrations Manager; Diana Bourdrez, Picture Editor; Matt Wascavage, Manager of Publishing Services; Sean Philpotts, Production Manager.

MANUFACTURING AND QUALITY MANAGEMENT
Christopher A. Liedel, Chief Financial Officer; Phillip L. Schlosser, Director; Clifton M. Brown III, Maryclare McGinty; Managers.

PROGRAM DEVELOPMENT
Gare Thompson Associates, Inc.

ART DIRECTION
Dan Banks, Project Design Company

CONSULTANTS/REVIEWERS
Dr. Margit E. McGuire, School of Education, Seattle University, Seattle, Washington

BOOK DEVELOPMENT
Nieman Inc.

BOOK DESIGN
Three Communication Design, LLC

PICTURE EDITING AND MANAGEMENT
Corrine L. Brock

MAP DEVELOPMENT AND PRODUCTION
Bruce Burdick

Published by the National Geographic Society
1145 17th Street, N.W.
Washington, D.C. 20036-4688

ISBN: 0-7922-4538-5

Fourth Printing November 2007
Printed in Canada

Cover: Quechua women walking an Inca trail
page 3 (top): Highway in Peru
page 3 (bottom): Wooden tiger head

CONTENTS

INTRODUCTION

Imagine living high among the peaks of the Andes Mountains in South America. You live in a community filled with gleaming objects made of gold. You help to build steep and narrow paths in the mountains. You are paid for your work in clothing or food. You might have done these things had you lived with the Inca **long ago**.

The Inca were a people who lived 500 years ago. The center of their **civilization** was the country that is now Peru.

Today, many visitors go to Peru to visit the ruins of an Inca city high in the clouds. In villages, they meet the modern relatives of the Inca. They discover that many of the old **traditions** are still a part of modern life in Peru.

There are amazing things to learn about the lives of the Inca. Let's begin a journey of our own.

Ruins of Machu Picchu, an Inca city in the clouds

PERU: THEN AND NOW

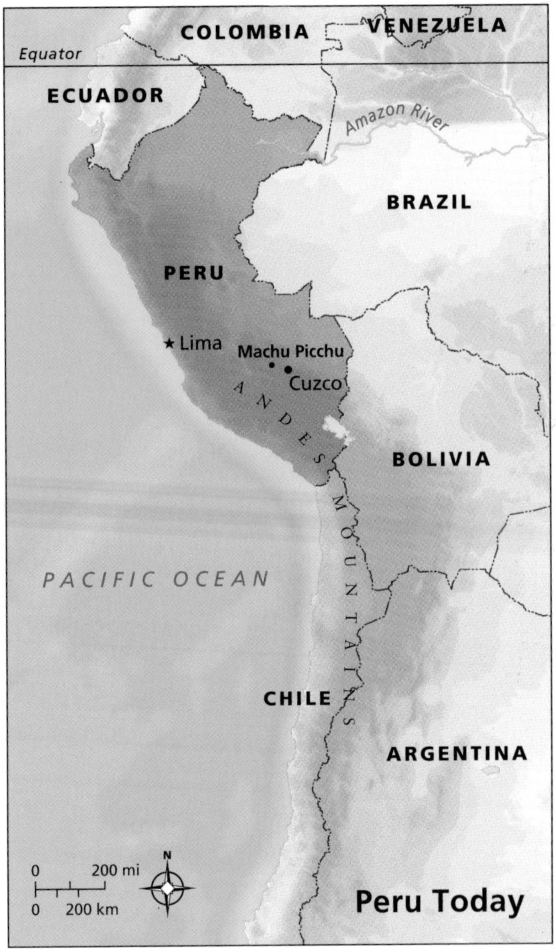

Around the year 1300, the Inca were a small group of people. During the next 200 years, Inca leaders fought wars. They defeated and ruled their neighbors. By 1500, more than 10 million people lived in the Inca empire.

The Inca empire stretched more than 2,000 miles (3,220 kilometers) down the west coast of South America. The great Inca empire no longer exists. It once ranged from present-day Ecuador into Chile.

Modern Cuzco

Cuzco long ago

Look at the first map. It shows the land that belonged to the Inca empire. The Inca capital was Cuzco (KOO-skoh). Find Cuzco on the map.

Now look at the second map. It shows the borders of modern Peru. What other modern countries are located on lands once ruled by the Inca? Peru's capital is Lima. Find Lima on the map.

Today, about half of Peru's people are descended from the Inca. They are the Quechua (KECH-wuh) people. Many of the Quechua speak Spanish, the official language of Peru. They also speak Quechua, the Inca language.

COMMUNITY LIFE

House with straw roof

HOUSES

Long ago, the Inca spent little time in their houses. Their houses were simple. People built them from stone and mud. They made the roofs from grass or straw. Most houses had one room with no windows. The floor was hard dirt.

Most families had no furniture. They slept on wool blankets, reed mats, or leather made from the skin of a **llama** (LAH-mah), an animal of the Andes Mountains.

Families sat on the floor to eat. They hung their few things on stone pegs. They kept their food in large jars and baskets. People cooked indoors. Fires were surrounded by stones set in a circle. The smoke drifted out through the grass roof.

Today, most Quechua people live in villages much like their ancestors did. Few families have electricity or running water. But these days, many have battery-operated radios!

Would you like making your own clothes? **Long ago**, clothes were made by hand. Inca women were wonderful weavers. They wove clothing from the wool of the alpaca, an animal related to the llama.

Men wore a cloth around the hips. It was held in place with a colorful belt. Many men also wore short tunics. Women wore long robes tied with a sash.

Everyone wore sandals. Men braided grass into slippers or used llama hide to make strong sandals. Some people wore gold disks in their earlobes. The more important the wearer, the larger the disk. The Inca ruler never wore the same thing twice.

Today, many Quechua men wear a modern shirt, trousers, and shoes. The weather is often cool. So, they might wear a woven poncho and a knitted cap with earflaps. Quechua women wear a knee-length full skirt. They tie a brightly woven cloth around their shoulders. Inside it, there might be a baby or a load of potatoes!

Quechua girls wearing wool ponchos

FOOD AND FARMING

What is your favorite snack? **Long ago,** an Inca might have chosen popcorn! Most of the time, people grew the food they ate.

Most Inca people were farmers, but farmland was scarce. Farmers had to create farmland on the mountainsides. To do this, they made terraces. First they built stone walls. Then they filled the area behind these walls with soil brought up from the river valleys.

They also dug irrigation channels to guide rainwater to their crops. Farmers planted maize, or corn, and quinoa (kih-NOH-uh), a grain native to the Andes. They also planted potatoes, beans, and chili peppers.

LOOKING BACK

Did you know that the first potato came from Peru? Today, there are over 200 kinds! They come in every size and shape. They are purple, pink, orange, red, white, or yellow. In ancient times, the Inca could freeze-dry potatoes. The potatoes could then be kept for a while.

A man and child plowing land for potatoes

Women selling fruits and vegetables at a market

The Inca had no animals to help remove rocks, plow the soil, or harvest crops. Their llamas weren't strong enough. So men, women, and teenagers did the work. Children tended the llama flocks.

Usually, the Inca cooked soups and stews with quinoa or potatoes. They roasted or boiled corn.

The Inca ate little meat. For feasts, they had llama, alpaca, or animals they hunted, such as deer, rabbits, and large birds. They also raised guinea pigs for food. They found them delicious when roasted with peanut sauce.

Today, many Quechua grow the same food their ancestors grew. Others raise grains introduced from other countries. They also eat fish from the ocean.

The Quechua go to town to buy, sell, and trade food at open-air markets. There they can get goods from other parts of Peru. They can also buy radios, cosmetics, and other things from the modern world. But they still eat guinea pig!

GROWING UP

Everyone had a job to do in the Inca world of **long ago**, even the children. For the first two years of a baby's life, it traveled everywhere on its mother's back. Not yet named, it was just called the Quechua word for "baby." A baby was given a name during his or her first haircut.

Noblemen's sons attended four years of school. Most children learned what they needed to know from their parents.

By the age of nine, children worked. Boys and girls helped in the fields and gathered firewood. Girls also spun yarn, dyed cloth, prepared food, and cared for younger children.

At the age of 14, boys were considered adults. Then, they were given their adult name. Girls married between the ages of 16 and 20. Boys married by age 25. Their partners were chosen for them.

Quechua mother and child

LOOKING BACK

In the Inca world of **long ago**, very young boys and girls learned to care for animals. **Today**, herding has declined, and children must attend school. In the country, some children, like this boy, watch over herds high in the mountains.

Quechua boy taking care of a herd of sheep

WORK AND TRAVEL

MONEY AND TAXES

The Inca had lots of gold, but they didn't use it for money. In fact, they had no money. They had to pay taxes, however. How would you pay taxes without money? You might pay with work. **Long ago**, Inca villagers had to pay taxes on their harvest and herds. Some of their crops and animals went to the empire.

Every village had to send a few young men and women to work for the empire. Some went to the capital to make jewelry, cloth, or pottery for nobles. Many men worked as soldiers or miners. Others built buildings or repaired roads or bridges.

The Quechua of **today** use money. They also trade goods. They are no longer ordered to leave their villages to work for the government.

LOOKING BACK

The Inca had no written language. Officials used a tool called a *quipu* (KEE-poo) to record how much property a village had. It was a bundle of knotted cords. For counting, officials tied knots in the cords. Different colored cords stood for different things, such as llamas or corn.

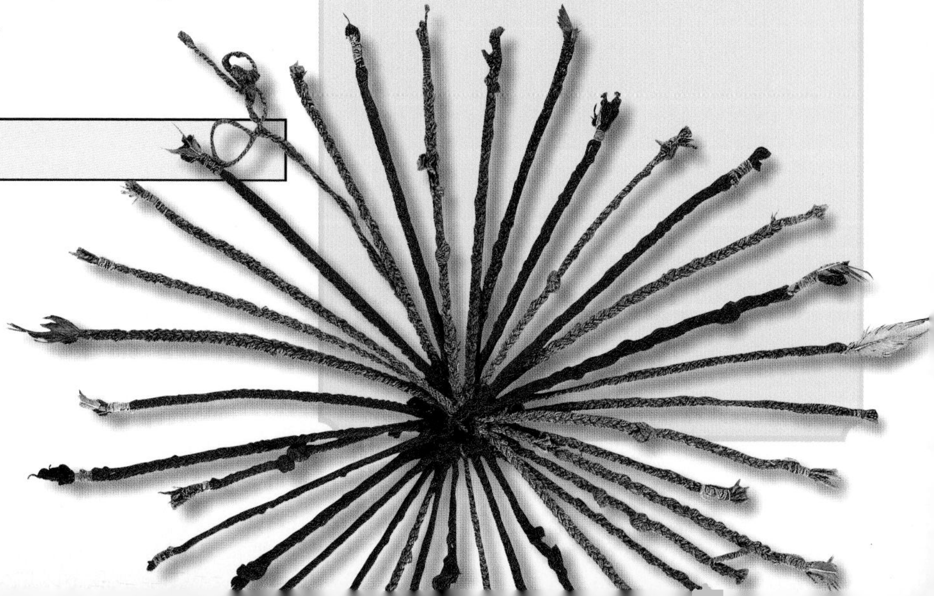

Inca quipu

ROADS AND BRIDGES

What would you do if there were no cars, trains, or planes? **Long ago**, the Inca had none of these things. They did not know about wheels. But they could walk! So they built thousands of miles of highways.

This amazing road system linked the villages of the empire with its capital at Cuzco. It was paved with stone. The Inca army marched thousands of miles on it. Officials on business traveled long distances too. Along the way, there were shelters every few miles. Canals lined the road so people could stop and get drinks of water.

The Inca also built bridges. Some bridges swayed above deep canyons. They were made of ropes of fiber from a type of cactus. Some ropes were as thick as a person's body!

Today, the 20-mile (32-kilometer) Inca Trail high in the Andes tests the legs of tourists. Every year, thousands of people travel to Peru to hike it.

Rope bridge

THE ARTS

Do you like to make things? Inca smiths, or metalworkers, made beautiful objects from gold and silver. They made masks, jewelry, vases, and cups. Because they made things for the nobles, the king gave them food, housing, and all the tools they needed.

Making cloth was another important craft. All Inca women could turn wool fleece from alpacas or vicuñas (vi-KOON-yuhs) into cloth. It was a long process. First, a woman had to work with a spindle. The spindle was a special stick used to twist fleece into yarn.

Once the yarn was dyed, weavers began to weave the yarn into cloth on a loom. They wove patterns of animals and people into the cloth. The patterns often told stories.

LOOKING BACK

The Inca mined huge amounts of gold and silver. They called gold "sweat of the sun" and silver "tears of the moon."

Inca gold sculpture of a toucan, a kind of bird

Today, Quechua girls, women, and some boys and men knit and weave belts, hats, bags, ponchos, and blankets. They use llama, alpaca, vicuña, and sheep wool. They make some things using the same tools as the Inca used. They also use modern looms and factory-made trimmings.

A poncho with traditional designs can take hundreds of hours to weave. A young Quechua man might expect to get one as a gift and wear it his whole life. Underneath the poncho, he wears jeans and a shirt.

Traditional Inca poncho

Modern Quechua weavers

GREAT CITIES AND RULERS

GREAT CITIES

In 1911, an archaeologist visiting Peru stood high in the Andes. He was staring in amazement at an old Inca city built on a mountaintop. No one from outside Peru had ever seen it before. It was the ruins of Machu Picchu (MAH-choo PEEK-choo).

Long ago, the Inca were skilled builders. Their tools were simple. They used axes, hammers, and chisels made of stone, wood, and bronze, a metal.

Yet Machu Picchu temples, palaces, houses, and roads were built of granite, a hard stone. How did the workers do it? Somehow, they carved enormous blocks and fit them together. The blocks fit so tightly that even a piece of paper could not slip between them. Earthquakes could not knock them down.

It took hundreds, maybe thousands, of men to move the biggest blocks of stone. They weighed up to 50 tons. How were they lifted? No one is sure.

Today, archaeologists are trying to solve the mysteries of Inca building. Luckily, many ancient walls in Cuzco, Machu Picchu, and other places are still standing.

Ancient walls in Machu Picchu still exist.

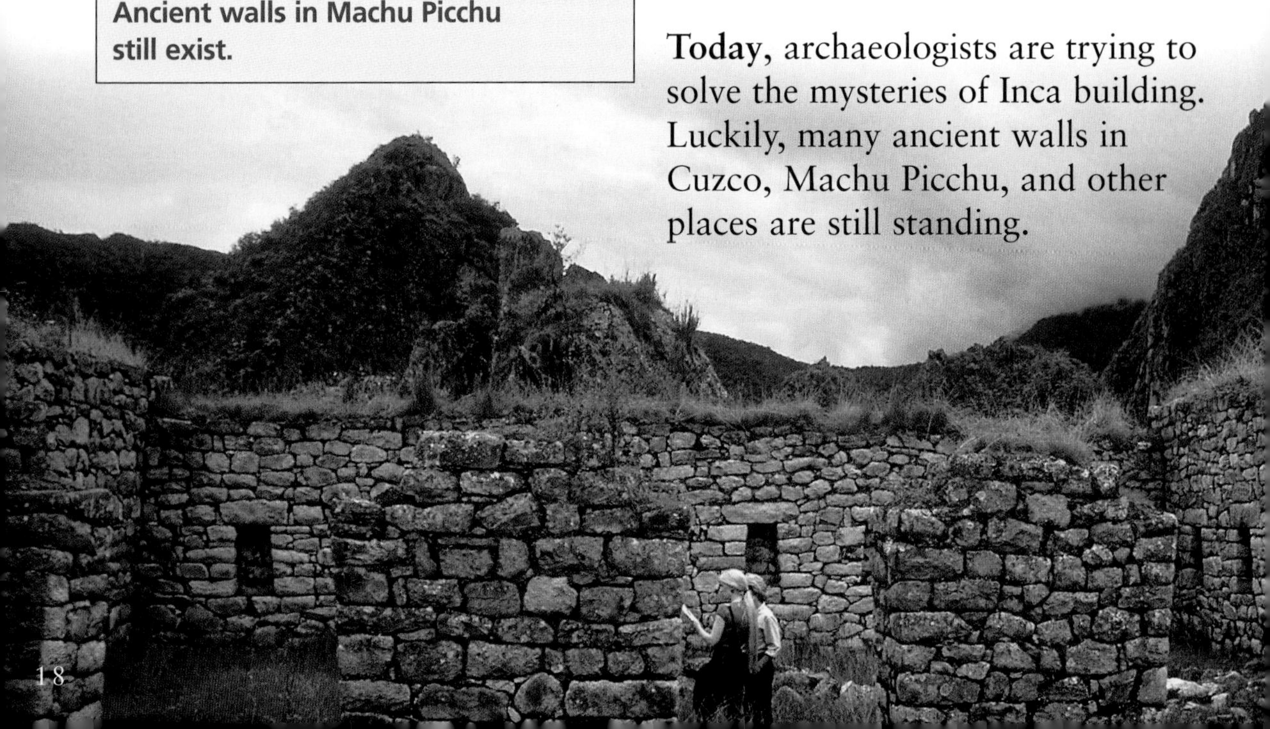

LOOKING BACK

In 1532, a small army from Spain attacked Cuzco with guns and horses. They wanted gold. They killed the Sapa Inca and made his people slaves. They took 11 tons of gold, melted it down, and shipped it back to Spain. Within 10 years, the Spanish had defeated the whole Inca empire.

This painting, from the walls of an old church in Lima, shows four Sapa Incas.

RULERS

Long ago, an Inca ruler traveled on a litter, a chair on poles. Men held it on their shoulders. He passed slowly, to impress everyone.

Each Inca ruler was called Sapa Inca, which means "only ruler." Each Sapa Inca built his own palace in Cuzco, where he sat on a gold throne. He was thought to be the child of the sun, and what he said was law.

The empire was well organized. It had a huge army and strict rules. Since breaking the law was usually punished with death, there were no jails. One of the most serious crimes was laziness. Lazy people who did not do their work were put to death!

Today, Peru has a president. People vote for officials to run the country. In the mountains, most Quechua also have village leaders.

CELEBRATIONS

Do you like to go to parties? What do you celebrate? **Long ago**, many Inca celebrations were religious. Priests and other people prayed and made offerings to the gods. They danced, sang, feasted, and told tales of Inca history. The festivals were like giant parties.

The queen of the Festival of the Sun rides on a litter.

Each month there were several feast days. Feasts were held to celebrate marriages and the time when young people became adults. Often there was also a major festival that might last for a week. There was even a festival to honor the dead.

Today, dances, parades, and other celebrations are popular in Peru. In Spanish, they are called *fiestas*. In Cuzco, one fiesta is a parade in honor of the Lord of the Earthquakes. Powerful earthquakes have destroyed whole villages in the Andes.

The Festival of the Sun is celebrated in winter, when the sun is at its lowest point in the sky. On that day, people walk from Cuzco to the ruins of the Inca fort outside the city. They follow actors dressed up as Sapa Inca and his guards. Of course, the king and queen ride high on royal litters! At the fort, everyone lights fires to bring back the sun.

THEN & NOW

Making music was important to the Inca. They played flutes made from bone or wood. They blew trumpets made from seashells. They beat drums made from animal skins. **Today**, the Quechua play the same types of instruments, as well as harps and guitars. The music of the Andes is popular around the world.

A boy plays a wind instrument.

CONTRIBUTIONS

Terraced fields at Machu Picchu

In fewer than 200 years, the Inca planned and built wonderful roads, bridges, and cities. They now amaze the world. Walking on the Inca Trail or looking at Machu Picchu today, we see how people lived long ago and how they solved problems.

Inca artists changed the world too. They made beautiful and useful things from metals, fibers, and clay. They wisely passed along their skills. One of the finest cloths today is made from alpaca wool. And the music and dances of the Inca enrich the culture of the Andes as well as the rest of the world.

The Inca were clever farmers. Their skills still teach people how to work with land, seasons, and climate. The Inca also gave the world many foods. Next time you eat a potato, tomato, pineapple, or peanut, remember who farmed it long ago!

Herd of alpacas

GLOSSARY

alpaca an animal with long, silky hair, or wool

archaeologist a person who studies the past by digging up old buildings and objects and examining them carefully

civilization a highly developed and organized society

descended came down from a certain family or group

empire a group of people or countries under one government or ruler

enrich make richer or more valuable

fleece wool that grows on a sheep or other similar animal

irrigation a way of supplying land with water

litter a couch or chair carried on the shoulders

llama a South American animal that has wooly hair. It is used to carry heavy loads.

loom a frame or machine for weaving yarn into cloth

poncho a large cloth worn as an outer garment with a slit in the middle for the head to go through

smiths people who make things from metal

spindle the rod or pin used in spinning to twist, wind, and hold thread or yarn

terraces flat, raised banks of earth, often made on a hillside to make spaces for growing crops

traditions customs, ideas, or beliefs passed down from parents to children

tunic a loose-fitting shirt or gown that reaches the knees

vicuñas wild animals of South America related to llamas. They have soft, silky fleece.

INDEX

Fortress ruins near Cuzco